YOUR
BRAIN
TO
EXTINGUISH
BURNOUT

52 Keys to Prevent, Break Through,
and Eliminate Burnout
(once and for all)

Published by jessICAREctor International

jessicarector.com

ISBN: 9781093945614

Cover design by: Okomota
Layout by: solfire@phoenix-farm.com
Cover photo by: Megan Weaver Photography

jessicarector.com

Dedication

Beastie,

It's still hard to believe you're gone. Someone will say something, I'll see a sign, or hear something on the radio and think of you. I look at B and wonder how much fun the two of you would have had together. He would've loved you so much. And you would've loved him so much.

Someone once asked me if I could have one last conversation with you, what would I say. My answer to that question led me down the path of helping others with their inner communication, their self-talk, and their mindset. And that's created massive changes, joy, and transformations with myself, B, and others.

jessicarector.com

You always believed in me. You always stood by me. You always got me. You would've loved what I'm doing now, and I know you're still supporting me (yelling my name out loud cheering me on) even from afar.

Thank you for giving me 39 years. I only wish I had more.

Love your younger sister,

Tease 'em

Preface

Since I started working at 15 years old, I've had many more jobs I didn't like than jobs I did. Let me clarify. I started out liking them okay, but as the newness soon wore off, I began to dread going to work. Hated going to work. Yet knew I needed to go to work.

I also hated looking for another job. I didn't like the idea of interviewing (not because I was bad at it, but I just didn't want to do everything it took to even get an interview), starting at the bottom, or having to learn how things were done at a different place.

So I stayed longer at jobs than I should have. The longer I stayed the more I disliked the job. I always did my job well and with a smile, yet I would have this feeling inside of me. You know the one that you can't put your finger on...

Looking back I realized I was burned out in many of those jobs and didn't even realize it. I didn't have a name for it. That feeling I couldn't put my finger on was misery and came from being burned out and it directly affected everything in my life, unbeknownst to me at the time.

Which is why I wrote this book. Not only have I been there, so I get it, but burnout is also one of my most requested programs. Burnout is on the rise, and it's not stopping.

In this book, you'll find my research on burnout (and it shows you'll soon be one of them without this book), strategies to prevent burnout, and tools to get out of that miserable state.

It's all about helping you to prevent, break through, and eliminate burnout so you don't have that misery engulfing your life like I did. Ready to prevent and extinguish burnout?

Let's get started!

JessICAREctor

Key 1

Burnout has to do with what's going on with you mentally and/or emotionally. It's not physical.

It can affect you physically (more fatigued, eating more, less exercise) but it begins and ends with your brain.

How can you help your mind?

What will it take to ignite, motivate, and empower (blaze) your brain?

Key 2

Brain breaks. Just like your body needs breaks from working out, so does your brain. It's constantly working (sometimes harder than other times). And in those times it's working hard, make sure you're taking frequent breaks.

Turn off your brain. Shut it down. Why? Because when you allow your brain a break, you allow it to re-energize. When you get back to it, you'll be more focused and present. You'll make fewer mistakes and better decisions.

Hint: Great ways to give your brain a break is to change your scenery or take a walk without getting on social media. Give yourself a mental break and turn off work mode.

Key 3

The Domino Effect: When dominoes are standing lined up and the first one falls, they all fall. This chain reaction happens in burnout too.

You don't wake up one day in burnout. It's a slow progression. Over time. Change happens at work. New leadership comes in. Coworkers leave. You're required to do more work in less time. A merger takes place. Longer hours. Less flexibility. More routines. Little time for fun, play, or creativity. Less and less appreciation. More and more demands.

One thing happens, and it becomes your new norm. Another thing happens, then that's your new norm. Then another and another. Before you know it, you're exhausted, stressed and burned out.

How are you taking care of you along the way to ensure you don't reach burnout?

Key 4

Burnout is a mental chain game.

The games we play in our head are linked with something else. So when you feel burnout in one area or in one aspect, it's linked to something else. Meaning it will directly affect something else.

Burnout affects areas of your life that may seem unrelated, yet everything is linked together.

Burnout at work is affecting you at home.

For example, here's one burnout chain. Burnout with your job lowers your performance, which means you have to stay late, which adds stress. That stress creates more irritability, less patience, and more frustration. So when your child asks you an easy question, you can simply snap without cause.

Then you feel guilty when you go to sleep, so you can't fall asleep. You wake up in a bad mood the next day. And the conversation with a client goes poorly or you don't make that sale with the prospect which impacts your pay/evaluations, and you wonder if you should get another job. And then...

The cycle never ends. It affects all areas of your life.

Key 5

Create your own mental chain game.

What is burnout affecting? Then what does that next thing affect?

Start with one thing or area that could use attention, help, or improvement.

Keep creating the chain and see how long it gets and the different areas it affects and hurts.

Key 6

According to my company's research, 79% of the workforce is burned out. And almost half are extremely burned out.

You'll likely be one of them at some point in your life or career.

So what are you doing to help prevent burnout?

Key 7

When you sleep, your brain recharges.

When you're not getting good, quality sleep, you're not allowing your brain to recharge. It leaves it wide open to negative thoughts (comparison, self-doubt, second guessing, bad attitude, perfectionism, not feeling good enough, criticizing).

They don't just come in and set up camp. They'll set up a whole campground, making it harder to be positive. Negative thinking is the #1 contributing factor to burnout. So when you don't get good quality sleep, you're more likely to feel burned out.

Key 8

Signs you might be heading to burnout...

- You're exhausted
- Never feel caught up
- Aren't getting good quality sleep
- Poor attitude
- Low morale or motivation
- Don't want to do anything
- Consistently stressed/feel pressure
- Don't feel good enough/worthy
- Catch yourself taking frequent breaks (coffee, bathroom, chatting), just so you don't have to work
- Procrastination
- Don't want to...go to work/home, deal with/be around certain people, resolve issues but instead ignore them

Key 9

What contributes to your burnout?

Contributing factors to burnout:

Overtime, too much work, inner communication/negative thoughts, not enough sleep, negative workplace, unfair compensation, workplace culture, perfectionism, bad habits, routines/boredom, poor leadership, lack of confidence, poor communication, not clear on company's vision, don't know your own purpose, and fear (fear of failure, fear of not being liked, fear of the unknown, fear of rejection, etc).

According to my company's research on the science of burnout, generally speaking across industries the top three contributing factors are perfectionism, routines/boredom, and bad habits, respectively.

What's your top contributing factor? What is one thing you can do to help so it doesn't contribute to burnout?

Key 10

What stresses you out? What are your triggers for stress?

Identifying your stress triggers allows you to be more proactive, instead of reactive. When you know what they are, you can see them from a mile away allowing you to anticipate and tackle them before they happen. When you wait for them to happen, you'll feel like you're backpedaling.

Key 11

Routines lead to burnout. Here's how to change up your routines...Your brain is super lazy. It lumps actions into one task.

Take for instance taking a shower. Your brain lumps it together as "taking a shower." It doesn't create it step by step. Turn on the water. Turn the nozzle to hot water. Pull the plug for the shower. Lift your leg up. Put your leg down to step into the shower. Turn your body around to the left and so on. If it had to think of all the steps, you'd be exhausted 10 minutes after you woke up.

Still, your brain needs to be challenged. It wants to think. Let it think by changing things up. Instead of washing your arm first, wash your leg first. Get two different soaps and have your brain decide which soap to use each time you shower. Small things get your brain working. When your brain works, it extinguishes burnout. So these small things create massive results.

Key 12

When you're feeling stress, pressure, or burnout, put on your favorite song and sing and dance. Whether you're breakdancing, doing the Running Man or the Robot, or just moving your shoulders: dance. Or sing at the top of your lungs (if you're at work, you can sing out loud softly).

I dare you.

If you put on your favorite song and it doesn't get you moving...if you don't dance or sing, then you need a new favorite song. ☺

Key 13

We put up gates for infants to keep them in a room, from climbing the stairs, or from getting out of bed. We create boundaries. As they get older, those boundaries become more flexible. They stay out later, be involved in more activities, and even drive.

As adults, boundaries almost cease to exist. We say Yes when we really want to say No. We allow others' opinions to outweigh ours. We put others' needs before our own.

Where do you need stronger boundaries in your life and work? When you don't want to do it, don't do it. Say No (yes, it's *that* easy). Set up a time to stop working and stick with it. Give yourself wind down and "me" time each day.

Boundaries are a necessity in order to accomplish what needs to be done and keep sane. Sounds simple, but are you doing it?! The more you do it, the better you get at doing it. Build better boundaries.

Key 14

A support system is vital for mental and emotional well being.

You need someone to support you inside and outside of work. Inside of work helps, so you have someone who gets it...who gets the job, your boss, the wins, the challenges, and the day to day stress. Someone in a similar situation.

Someone outside of work is also necessary so you can peel away work. If all you do is talk about work, then that will continue to add stress, pressure, and burnout to your life. You need someone who you don't have to talk about work with, that you can decompress with and just fully be you...goofy, fun, let go, easy going, stress free you.

Where do you need more support (inside or outside of work)?

From whom do you need better support?

Key 15

When people get busy or stressed, the first thing they take out of their lives is fun. And that's the one thing you need in your life in those situations. Fun and play liven up your day and reduce burnout. When you play more, you use your imagination which leads to more creativity and innovation.

Add some fun and play into your day to re-energize your spirit and spice up your daily routines.

Where can you add fun and play to your days? Who do you want to spend more time with playing and having fun? What type of play or fun do you want to have (be specific)? When will you start?

Hint: The more specific you are (list the person, where, when, and what you want to do), the more likely you are to actually do it.

Key 16

Success with stress is about knowing how to adjust, change, and tweak along the path so you never reach burnout (again). The more you think about something, the more you think about it. *Duh, Jessica.*

What I mean is the more you think about it, the more you'll continue to think about it. Stress is just something not meeting your expectations. So the more you think it's not meeting your expectations, the more stressed you get. The more you think about the stress, the more stress you continue to pile on. When you're feeling stressed, what do you need (or what do you need to change) in order to reduce the stress? Either lower your expectations or ask yourself why it's not meeting your expectations. Then find a solution for why it isn't meeting your expectations.

Hint: The solution is in the questions you ask and the way you're asking the questions.

Key 17

Puzzles and games build brain muscles. They work both your left and right sides of the brain, and they get you thinking in new and different ways.

When your brain is being challenged, it's doing something new and different. Something it's not used to doing. And in the process, it's exciting; therefore, burnout won't occur.

Pick up a crossword puzzle, Sodoku, or a brain teaser.

Get a group of colleagues, peers, or friends to play Pictionary, Running Charades, or Scattergories with you.

The more you play, the more burnout ceases to exist. And having fun is a wonderful bonus.

Key 18

What would you do if you were in financial bankruptcy?

You could...

Get a loan, ask for help, or live with family or friends.

Burnout is emotional and mental bankruptcy.

You wouldn't sit and do nothing with financial bankruptcy. You can't afford to sit and do nothing with burnout.

Just like with financial bankruptcy, burnout won't go away on its own. You have to choose to do something to resolve it. How can you be proactive about burnout?

Key 19

Exercise is known to relieve stress. It builds your mind as it tones your muscles.

Stretch, walk, run, dance, ride a bike.

Get up.

Get out.

MOVE. YOUR. BODY.

Key 20

Don't power through. You have a project, deadline, or something you want to finish, you power through. You go, go, go, just to get it done.

This is one of the worst things you can do.

By doing this, you're doing yourself a disservice, because you're less productive. You become more easily distracted and less focused leading to lower performance, inefficiency, and more mistakes. To be the most productive, cut yourself a break...and give yourself a few breaks. Work 50 minutes, take a 10 min break, work 50 minutes, take a 10 min break.

Doing this allows your energy, motivation, and focus to increase. You'll be able to get more things done faster and correctly.

Key 21

What's your why?

Why do you do what you do?

If you've been doing it for a while, it's easy to lose sight of the reason why you started doing it in the first place. Get back to the core reason for doing it, the difference you are making, and the big picture.

When you get bogged down by the details and the minutiae, you forget to focus on the bigger picture and the impact you're making. Put a spotlight on your impact, and you'll realize the other things just don't matter to the bigger mission, vision, and purpose.

Key 22

What is your self care routine? How are you taking care of *you*?

Put your mask on you first before you can take care of others. You can't be the best spouse, parent, friend, or child if you aren't taking care of yourself. You'll keep going, going, going taking care of everyone else but you. It's time for you to take care of you! Make sure your needs are being met.

It's not once a week; it's every day. How can you take better care of yourself? What do you need in order to do that?

What is one thing you will do to take care of yourself today?

Key 23

Psychologists say that once you reach midlife, 95% of your day is routine. That leaves only 5% for flexibility.

You have routines inside your routines.

Think of your routines. You go to the same restaurants. Sit in the same place at the table. You likely either sit facing the door or away from the door, but it's the same even if you're at a different table. Order the same things.

Change up your routines.

What is one thing you can do that's different, new, or fresh?

Key 24

Growth only happens outside your comfort zone.

Burnout only happens inside your comfort zone.

One way to extinguish burnout: Find a way to grow, learn, and develop, for these are like water on the flame of burnout.

A few ideas are to take a course, get a mentor, lead a team, or start a business.

What can you do to grow, learn, and develop in one area of life?

Key 25

In the midst of burnout, it's not about being resilient.

Resiliency, according to Dictionary.com means "to recover quickly from difficult situations."

You don't want to linger in burnout; however, you do want to process burnout. Why are you in burnout? What led to being burned out? What will help you extinguish burnout?

Popping out of burnout or recovering quickly doesn't allow you to review your burnout. Without reviewing it, you won't know how to prevent it from happening again. So being resilient in the face of burnout guarantees you one thing...the same thing happening again and that next time you'll reach burnout faster and deeper.

Working through burnout is not about resilience. It's about finding out what you need to be more equipped and better prepared.

Key 26

Your brain is constantly working. Give your brain a break. ☺

Let it relax, re-energize, and rejuvenate by shutting off for a few minutes. Meditate, put your head back and close your eyes, or go on a walk.

Beat burnout by taking several mini breaks to:

- Keep your energy high
- Remain focused
- Stay active
- Be engaged
- Stay motivated

jessicarector.com

Key 27

Blaze Your Balance Wheel

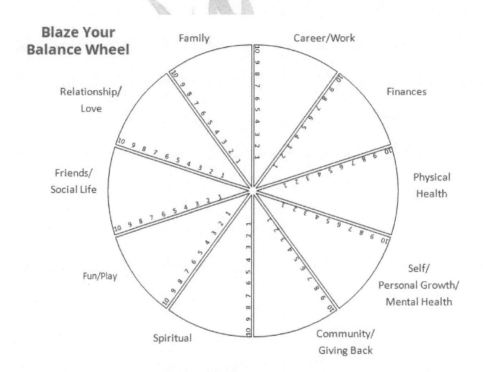

Blaze Your Balance Wheel

Family

Career/Work

Relationship/ Love

Finances

Friends/ Social Life

Physical Health

Fun/Play

Self/ Personal Growth/ Mental Health

Spiritual

Community/ Giving Back

jessicarector.com

There are 10 areas of your life. It's unrealistic to expect yourself to do amazingly well in all areas. When one area isn't that great, it's easy to beat yourself up about it. Not meeting high expectations leads to burnout, which creates a cycle. High expectations. You're not living up to them. You get stressed. You're burning out which creates more expectations you're not living up to.

Instead of doing that, let's look at it as an opportunity. Where can I be doing better? What do I need to improve in that area just a bit?

Key 28

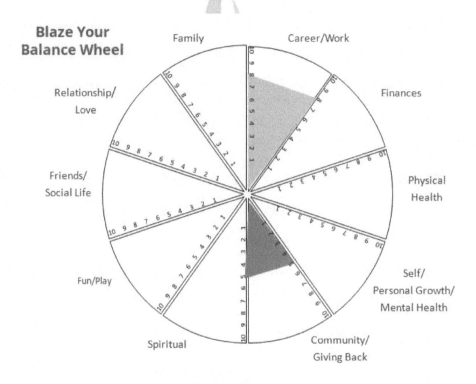

Blaze Your Balance Wheel

Family

Career/Work

Relationship/Love

Finances

Friends/Social Life

Physical Health

Fun/Play

Self/Personal Growth/Mental Health

Spiritual

Community/Giving Back

jessicarector.com

Rate yourself in each area. It's not about marking down where you want to be. Put down where are you **right now**. Be honest. Number how you're doing in each area. Now find that number in the area and color in everything below that. So every category should have some portion colored in. If you are a 5 in Family, then color 5 and below in that category. **In which category do you want to improve?**

Hint: Be specific. The more specific you are, with whom, when, where, and how you will start, the more likely you are to actually do it. It's not about raising it to a 10, it's about moving it up one point. Which area will you focus on? What will you do in that area to increase it?

Key 29

You have mundane tasks that need to get done. Filing, data work, calls made, paperwork, proposals, or emails sent. Laundry, mowing the lawn, dishes, cleaning, running errands, kids' sports, or making meals.

Mundane tasks lead to burnout.

What can you do to turn mundane tasks into fun?

You can turn anything into a game. Challenge yourself to beat your own time. Get a friend to play along where you race each other (if you have someone else, you can always turn anything into a race) or who will come up with the most creative ways of doing it. Put on music and dance and sing your way through it. Give yourself a prize for getting through it, beating your time, or doing it without errors.

Key 30

A fantastic way to reduce stress is to calm your breathing.

Whether it's before a meeting, a presentation, a challenging conversation, or a pressure filled situation, try boxed breathing and you'll find peace.

Here's how it works:

Think of a box, where all the sides are equal. You'll do this in beats of four. Breathe in for four beats, pause for four beats, breathe out for four beats, and pause for four beats. Repeat. In, pause, out, pause. Do it over and over, until your breathing is at an even pace, your heart rate slows, and your nerves disappear. The longer you do it, the better it'll work. Just make sure you're not so relaxed that you fall asleep ☺

Key 31

One of the top contributing factors to burnout is bad habits.

Here are some examples:

- Checking email/social media
- Working through lunch
- Not scheduling time for yourself
- Filling your calendar with too much
- High expectations
- Always in work mode
- Hiding your emotions during meetings/with your team/with those closest to you

Which one do you do? What can you implement to change this bad habit?

Hint: In order to lighten burnout, the change will need to be consistent. Doing something different one time won't create a long-term solution.

Key 32

Calm your mind and body.

Find peace within yourself, whether it's meditation or just closing your eyes to turn off your mind.

Stress is really about how things aren't measuring up to expectations. Something not living up to expectations, needs, or wants.

When you turn off your thoughts, you stop thinking. When you do that, the stress subsides.

What isn't measuring up to your expectations?

Key 33

Create boundaries with those you love.

You walk in the door and before you take a step inside, you're bombarded. A child needs help finding something. Someone else wants help with homework. While someone else is asking what's for dinner.

Can you get a quick break first?!

You need time to decompress. So educate those you love on what *you* need. Let them know you need a few minutes. Walk in your room. Sit on your bed. Let go of the stress, worry, and pressure from the day. Change your clothes.

When you come out, you're all theirs. After all, you want to hear what they have to say, and be 100% focused and present for them.

Key 34

Make sure to educate those you love about your boundaries.

They can't read your mind.

If you don't educate them, the same thing will keep happening. And there will come a day, when you snap, yell, or raise your voice to them. Then it'll likely happen again.

They will stop coming up to you asking for your help. They will stop communicating with you or greeting with hugs, because they won't know the mood you'll be in. They received the snapping response before, and they don't like how it made them feel, so they will just stop approaching you.

Ensure they don't feel like they are walking on eggshells around you, educate them. Be patient, as with anything that is new, it takes time to adjust and for the habit to take hold.

Key 35

Don't work through lunch. Your brain needs that time to unwind, relax, and recharge.

Shut off your brain.

Decompress. Talk to a friend, take a cat nap, or read a book. Let your brain let loose for a minute.

When you get back to work, you'll find yourself more focused, energized, and productive.

Key 36

Stop thinking so hard.

Ever forgotten the name of a song or someone's name? Then several hours later, when you're doing something else, all of a sudden it pops into your head.

It's because you stopped pushing your brain so hard to think of it.

When you allow your brain to step away and relax, the answers come to you.

Problems get solved, decisions get made, and issues get resolved.

Key 37

Knowing vs. Doing

Some of these things you might have heard before. You may even "know" them, but are you doing them? And are you doing them consistently?

There is a difference between knowing and doing. When you do them, that's the only way you'll see the impact, results, and outcomes. The only way you'll create change and get out of burnout is when you implement changes into your life and work.

And it's not about just doing them. You have to ensure you're doing them on a constant and continual basis to ensure burnout doesn't resurface.

What is one thing that you might know but now you'll implement to make change happen?

Key 38

Burnout Life Cycle

The longer you're in a profession or at a job, the more often you'll face burnout, the longer it will last, and the harder it is to get out of it.

Most of the time people don't know what to look for to know if burnout is about to hit. They barely recognize it when they are *in* it, because it's such a slow progression. Once they are in it, they try to dig themselves out of it.

What are you doing to ensure it doesn't hit?

Key 39

Chart Your Burnout Part 1

In each month, draw a dot at the number that best represents how you feel in relation to being burned out. A 10 means you have no burnout. You feel great! A 0 means you're in extreme burnout. Then draw a line connecting the dots. This gives you a visual representation of your burnout throughout the year.

Hint: When you do this each year, you will start to see patterns. It will allow you to create your own burnout life cycle and be more proactive with your stress, well being and overall health.

jessicarector.com

Key 40

Chart Your Burnout Part 2

This long-term strategy allows you to track where you are in burnout, from month to month. That way you can know which months you're more prone to burnout. Then you can be proactive.

If your busy time is summer and you tend to get burned out at the end of Aug, then you know in May, before your busy time hits, you need to schedule something revitalizing at the end of Aug.

A weekend getaway, a spa day, a friend outing, a guy trip. It'll give you something to look forward to and focus on instead of concentrating on your stress and never ending, busy, to-do list. When you have something scheduled ahead of time, you don't give burnout a chance of occurring or setting in.

Key 41

Routines lead to you being burned out and in a rut. Nothing needs to be routine.

Think of your sneakers. You've probably tied your shoes ten thousand plus times. They are probably laced up the same way they've been laced up since you were five-years-old first learning how to tie your shoes.

How can you lace up your sneakers differently? There are several different ways to do it. Let your brain start working in new and creative ways.

Creativity and innovation conquers burnout EVERY.SINGLE.TIME! How can you introduce more creativity and innovation into your days, work, and projects?

Key 42

What are your two favorite hobbies or activities that you do on a weekly or monthly basis?

It's okay if you don't know. When adults are asked this question, most people can't name two, because they get so caught up with work and family they forget to take time out to enjoy their own hobbies or activities.

Take time each daily, week, or month to enjoy your favorite things. Paint. Have a spa treatment. Golf. Hula Hoop. Go to a play. Rock climb. Go water rafting. Play laser tag. Do a ropes course. Write a song.

Find. Discover. Explore. Do the things you enjoy the most to ignite the fire inside of you again.

Key 43

Negative thinking (like perfectionism) is the #1 contributing factor to burnout, according to my company's research. Why?

Because they keep you stagnant, in your comfort zone, and repeating the same patterns. Negative thinking keeps that same self-talk spinning like...

- I don't know for sure how to do that
- I don't want to look dumb (stupid, fat, not attractive, like I'm an amateur)
- I can't put myself on camera
- I'm not sure what to say on the call
- It's not going to be good

Burnout happens when you stay in the same place for too long. The more you think about being perfect, the more you'll continue to think about it and the less action you will take.

Stop trying to be perfect.

jessicarector.com

No one connects with perfection.

Get out there and just do it.

Try. Try. Try. Try.

Then try some more.

Eventually you'll get good. Then great.

Perfectionism holds you back from learning, growing, and flourishing. Let go of perfectionism so you can move to the next level.

Throw perfectionism out the window and embrace the amazing, imperfect, willing to try YOU.

Key 44

Stop thinking so much.

Think less. Achieve more!

You tend to think the same thoughts over and over. It's ingrained in the thinking process.

Imagine more, innovate more, and create more. You will invigorate the brain with new ideas, ways, and thoughts.

It disrupts the brain's status quo, which also disrupts burnout. So, let your mind go free with the possibilities.

Key 45

Games allow your brain to grow and flourish. And they are a lot of fun.

What's a mundane task (at home or work) that you need to do? How can you make it into a game?

This adds more fun into something that is often boring and creates some excitement to turn that something you don't want to do into a something you don't mind doing.

> Think laundry, dishes, filing, paperwork, making calls, cleaning, proposals, end of day must-do activities.

Key 46

How does burnout affect you?

My company's research shows that 76% of people say burnout affects their self-talk, motivation, attitude, and performance. And since these things directly impact burnout, it's a vicious cycle.

Your self-talk is at the foundation of your attitude, motivation, and performance, yet most of the time you don't recognize it even exist.

You must interrupt this pattern to stop the cycle; otherwise, burnout will continue to exist and take over your life (without your realizing it is).

Key 47

Smile.

It sounds so simple and it is. How often are you doing it?

It's something you have to consciously think about.

It's almost impossible to smile and still be in a bad mood or to feel burned out, at least in that moment.

It'll keep you from being in a poor mood or having a bad attitude.

When you have to show up for something or someone, and you're just not feeling like it, whether it's for a client, a meeting, or to work, smile. It's a short-term solution to burnout. It'll get you through the immediate moment. This minute. This hour. And sometimes that's all you need right now.

Key 48

Identify your stressors and triggers.

Is it a person, place, situation, or experience?

Be specific.

When you know them, you can recognize them before your stress levels increase. Then you can be proactive and decide what to do, whether it's walking away, not engaging, or getting right to the issue (and not procrastinating).

When you're able to do this, you'll tackle them before they are able to cause more stress, health issues, or burnout.

Key 49

What is one thing you've wanted to do that you haven't yet?

Go try it.

The ho hum every day, same ol' stuff, leads to boredom, which leads to burnout. Do something different. Something new. Something fun. Create your kind of adventure—add some spice to your life. Make the time to do it, because we have time for the things we want time for. What is it that's longing inside of you to do? If you can't think of something, take a moment to ponder this.

Start a list of things you want to do. Each week, each month, or each quarter make sure you do one thing. And when you do that one thing, make sure you're adding another thing to the list.

It's a Revolving List of Fun.

Key 50

You might have heard about the boiling frog. If you put a frog in boiling water, the frog will jump out. If you put the frog in warm water, the frog will stay in. He'll think, *Oooo, this feels good*. You slowly make the water hotter. He keeps thinking, *Ooooo, this feels good.*

He gets used to the warmer water. Then you turn the water up even more. He still thinks it feels good. You keep turning it up, and he keeps thinking it feels good. So when it does get to boiling temperatures, he won't recognize it as dangerously hot water.

The same thing happens with burnout. One new thing gets implemented and you think, *This isn't* soooo *bad*. It's your new norm. Then another thing gets implemented. This isn't so bad. It becomes your norm.

Things slowly get piled on. Then before long, you're in burnout.

Key 51

When you compare yourself to others (and not having what others have), you begin to subconsciously think you're not good enough or worthy. So the more you compare yourself to what someone else has, the more you'll think you don't measure up, which will keep you stuck and stagnant, which leads to feeling burned out.

Comparison doesn't serve you. In fact, it hurts you.

Instead of comparing situations, ask yourself, "What is it that they have that I want?"

Then ask, "What will it take to get it? Am I willing to do that?"

Find out what you need to do to achieve more (be more successful, make a bigger difference, find a job you love) or whatever it is you're wanting.

Be focused and disciplined to create it.

Key 52

Life can take its toll. It can become easy to get burned out, whether it's at your job, in a role, or being around the same people. Routines will also create burnout. Doing the same things day after day. Implement something to spice up your life.

Create	Explore	Celebrate
Build	Risk	Live
Discover	Enjoy	Develop

Monthly. Weekly. Daily. Do something to get out of the same ol' same ol'. Paint, start a company, pick up a sport, meet new friends, move to the beach or another state. Your initial response may be, "I can't, because..." and then a list of all the reasons why you can't. But...

YES. YOU. CAN!

It's your life...start creating the one you really want. So when you look back, you'll say, "I did some amazing things. I *REALLY* lived."

BLAZIN' ADVICE:

Since the release of *Blaze Your Brain to Extinguish Burnout,* I've had the opportunity to work with organizations, and I've found that:

1. Most organizations aren't doing much, if anything, to help their people with burnout.
2. People don't like admitting they are burned out for fear of how it will make them look or what their bosses (people who like to believe they are leading when, in fact, they aren't leading at all) will say or think.
3. Burnout affects most people on some level, no matter how small it is. The small level, over time, grows into bigger issues and challenges unless addressed at the small level.
4. Organizations don't know how to recognize burnout (they think it's other issues when it's really burnout).
5. When organizations do recognize burnout, they think it will go away on its own (and it won't).
6. Most people don't know the real cause of burnout, they think it's something it isn't.

WHAT BARRIERS WILL KEEP YOU FROM BLAZIN' YOUR LIFE:

In order to make a change in your burnout situation, you must implement the strategies discussed in this book. There are several obstacles that can keep you from implementation.
Here are the top 3:

1. You don't read the whole book. You read one or two keys and stop. It's imperative that you read it all. One strategy may not resonate with you, and the rest you may love. Give yourself the opportunity to work through the whole book.

2. Don't try something once and then forgo it. You've got to put a strategy into action and allow it to work over time. Just like you didn't learn to drive a car perfectly the first time. A new strategy and habit takes time to learn, develop, and grow.

3. Feeling shame or guilt around burnout. Most people have experienced it at least once. So let go of what you think others will say or think about it. That will just hold you back from working your way through it.

jessicarector.com

HOW TO GET THE MOST OUT OF THIS BOOK:

1. Finishing the book. If you read it all in one or two settings, go back and implement one key a week. That way you are consistently thinking about, implementing, and working through something to help you with burnout. You'll never feel stuck or stagnant doing this. When stress comes up, you'll have an immediate way to work through it.

2. Be patient with yourself. You're not going to be perfect from the beginning. Give yourself grace to find out what works best for you. It may not work first thing in the morning but may work better at midday. Give yourself the time to figure it out.

3. Take the strategies you learn from this book and share them with your organization, leaders, and team. If you're experiencing burnout, someone around you likely is too. Help them. Then you all can work through it together and make a bigger impact to your lives, families, and work.

MORE FROM

JESSICA RECTOR

SPEAKING

"Remarkable! Tremendous! Life Changing! You exceeded my expectations! You are truly an amazing motivational speaker, and I highly recommend you."
— Patti, meeting planner.

Thought Leader Jessica Rector is known for her high energy, engaging, and entertaining presentations. If you're looking for a boring, snoozer speaker, she is not it! Whether she's doing the Running Man in heels, showing a video of her son climbing the refrigerator, or interacting with attendees on stage, she has the uncanny ability to immediately connect with audiences making her a memorable and in-demand speaker.

She changes the game with her rare combination of vulnerability, substance, and humor. Jessica uses her company's research to

jessicarector.com

ignite people, performance, and profits and extinguish burnout and is known for creating change on the spot.

Audiences love her research and takeaways and the games they play during her sessions. Their focus, retention, and engagement increase. And as a bonus, they have a lot of fun.

She's works with teams, leaders, and organizations like NBCUniversal, the Dallas Mavericks, and American Airlines to transform their negative thoughts into positive action through her programs Blaze Your Brain: The Power of Self-Talk.

Jessica is a sure-fire win with audiences in any industry because she focuses on what makes us human: then allows us to exceed our potential in business and life and overcome what holds us back or stops us from achieving it. She tailors all presentations to the needs of the audience.

If you're looking for strong takeaways, audience interaction, and a lot of fun, book Jessica today (817) 523-1529.

jessicarector.com

TRAINING

Jessica helps organizations improve performance, communication, and leadership, while reducing turnover, stress and burnout.

Jessica knows everything begins with your inner game and has found most organizations don't usually teach strategies around that. They focus on the job duties, functions, or responsibilities which leaves open huge opportunities for organizations to help better their people.

Jessica specifically designs training, in person or online, for corporations, companies, and organizations who want their teams, staff, or executives to move to the next level. These solutions can be

jessicarector.com

formatted and tailored into a half day, a full day, monthly, or longer sessions to fit your needs and specifications.

In order to create massive change, it takes constant learning. Jessica also offers video series, monthly or weekly, for your people to continually learn and improve.

CONSULTING

Jessica works with companies who want to create massive change. She helps organizations identify how much money they are losing due to burnout, negative thoughts, and poor attitudes and develops personalized programs to decrease this loss through preventing, breaking though, and eliminating burnout for their teams and leaders.

Since burnout affects various aspects of lives, she works to tailor her consulting programs to each organization's needs, ensuring everyone's needs are met from employees to executives.

She's known to create massive results that transfer to other departments, improving bottom-line results throughout the organization.

jessicarector.com

FOR MORE INFORMATION:

For speaking inquiries, training, or consulting, please go to
jessicarector.com
or call Jessica directly at (817) 523-1529

Tame Your Brain Game: 52 Tips to Turn Negative Thoughts into Positive Action

In this transforming book, Jessica Rector, a thought leader on self-talk, walks you through your negative thoughts and how their impacting your life and gives you strategies to turn them into positive action for better results. Your inner conversations, what you say to yourself about yourself, is the foundation for everything in your life, at work, and in relationships. Jessica gives you proven steps, which have helped thousands, to take action and create massive change. These tips work for anyone, anytime, and anywhere. If you're ready to improve your work, relationships, and life, uplevel yourself, or create a change, no matter how big or small, this is a must-have book. Get your copy today!

jessicarector.com

The Adventurs of B Man: Blaise Your Brain

Five-year-old Blaise, aka B Man, takes you on the fun and enlightening ride in his first book. He motivates, inspires, and empowers you to life a life you enjoy while having the courage to be yourself. This book became a #1 best-seller within minutes of being published. Adults and kids alike are learning, growing, and transforming from taking to heart and implementing the tips B Man shares in this one-of-a-kind book. Join B Man as he takes you through fun, excitement and a lot of laughs that only he can do. So buckle up, put on your cape, and enjoy the wild ride with The Adventures of B Man. Get Ready to Blaise Your Brain! Book #2 in this series will be out in 2019.

jessicarector.com

Breaking the Silence: Taking the SH(hh) Out of Shame-#1 Best-Selling Book

"Powerful, insightful, and life changing! Jessica helps you get to the core of what's holding you back to reach more confidence and success faster. This book is a must read for anyone who is ready to break through barriers to live an extraordinary life and become their best." — Chris Widener, New York Times Best-Selling Author

In this ground-breaking #1 best-selling book, Jessica Rector takes you on a journey to uncover how shame has been holding you back at work and home and what it takes to create a solid foundation on which to create a life you love. In just five steps, from recognizing shame to knowing how to confront it when it comes up again, Jessica gives you a blueprint for lasting results. This book helps you release your shame, speak your voice, and stand in your power.

jessicarector.com

Life Defining Moments From Bold Thought Leaders- #1 Best-Selling Book

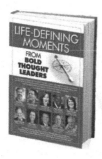

"Make your trip to a great life infinitely easier by reading, absorbing, and obtaining all the best that life offers. It is an awesome resource to help you have more love, abundance, joy, and fulfillment by living your life passionately on-purpose." — Mark Victor Hansen, Co-Creator of World's Best-Selling Book Series, Chicken Soup for the Soul

In this #1 best-selling book, Jessica Rector demonstrates pure vulnerability when she digs deep and shares her life-altering story that found her into the depths of despair. She also guides you through her journey of how that propelled her into transforming the lives of others, speaking on stages in front of thousands, and discovering and living her mission. Jessica was able to catapult her pain into something much bigger than herself, and by sharing her story, she empowers you to do the same.

jessicarector.com

Live Your Greatest Life Book

"This book shows you how to unleash your full potential for love, health, happiness, and complete fulfillment in life." — Brian Tracy, Motivational Speaker and author of *Change Your Thinking, Change Your Life*

Through the six steps to living the life you've always wanted, this book guides you to step out of your rut, get out of your own way, and leap to your future. It motivates and inspires you through real world examples to be who you are meant to be and reach your potential. This engaging book walks you through the processes of increasing your self-confidence, loving yourself, and becoming your authentic self. Jessica provides a step-by-step process to find your passion, confront your fears, and explore what you really want in life. It's time to stop settling for less than you deserve. It's time to take action to get it. This empowering guide has shown thousands of people the tools and techniques to make the change they want and need in their lives today. You are destined for more greatness. Get this book and achieve it today!

jessicarector.com

Live Your Greatest Life Journal

Create change and take massive action fast, when you know how to move forward. Writing is one of the most therapeutic and liberating things you can do for yourself. Sometimes you don't know the questions to ask yourself to get unstuck or to make forward progress. This journal guides you each step of the way. It asks you the tough questions, most you probably don't know to ask yourself, and gives you the space to find your way to the answers. Bottling your thoughts up just holds you back, so this journal allows you to release them in an organized and fluid way. With this journal, you will dig deep, stretch yourself, and make forward progress through the Live Your Greatest Life book faster while keeping track of your thoughts, ideas, and goals.

jessicarector.com

The BS Quote Book
Breaking The Silence: Taking The Sh(hh) Out Of Shame Quote Book

The BS Quote Book shares some of the BS you tell yourself that holds you back and how to change it to get what you want most. Sometimes we need that extra push, motivation, or inspiration to get us through or that reiteration that "I'm not the only one." This mini book is ideal for that and has the best of the best thoughts, quotes, and lessons from the best-selling book *Breaking the Silence: Taking the Sh(hh) Out of Shame.* It's perfect to put it in your pocket or purse, send as a gift, or hand out to inspire others.

This book is often bought in bulk to share as a gift for team members, clients, or friends.

jessicarector.com

This Man Thing Quote Book

For, about, and with men from all over the world. Start your day off right with wise, powerful insight from This Man Thing Quote Book. Inspired by men in This Man Thing Facebook group, this mini book is filled with empowering advice, feedback, and lessons from men to help other men through challenges, issues, or struggles and to let them know they are not alone. This book was created in hopes it might help, support and transform the lives of millions of men. It is perfect for you or the men in your life as a gift, to inspire others or to keep in your pocket for daily inspiration.

This book is often bought in bulk to share as a gift for team members, clients, or friends.

jessicarector.com

ABOUT THE AUTHOR

Jessica Rector's mission is simple: Transform Lives.

As the top female mindset and burnout expert, Jessica is the authority on tackling your inner game and turning it into outer success and positive action! She is known for her rare combination of energy, entertainment, and enthusiasm, making her a dynamic, Must See presenter. Whether she is doing the Running Man or interacting with participants on stage, audiences love her because she's innovative, impactful, and interactive and often considered as the best at the conference.

Before becoming one of the top motivational performance speakers, Jessica was a TV talk show host, an award winning #1 top sales performer at a Fortune 100 company, and a broadcaster. She knows firsthand how to turn your thoughts into massive business and life results. She uses her company's research, experiences, and

jessicarector.com

strategies to help organizations, leaders, and teams fire up their thinking, extinguish burnout, and ignite their people through her process called Blaze Your Brain: the Self-Talk Advantage.

Jessica has three college degrees, including an MBA, and has written eight books. As a #1 best-selling author, she has worked with clients such as NBCUniversal, the Dallas Mavericks, and American Airlines. Jessica is a Contributor for The Huffington Post and has been seen on ABC, NBC, CBS, FOX, and Business Journal for creating change.

Jessica also enjoys learning about the exciting world of Transformers so she can carry on real conversations with her five-year-old son, Blaise, who is a #1 best-seller author and the youngest published author in the United States.

For speaking engagements, training, or consulting, please go to jessicarector.com for more information.